Mental
Hospital

How to

Get Out

of a

Mental
Hospital

How to

Get Out

of a

Mental

ALSO BY
PHILLIP FRAGILE:

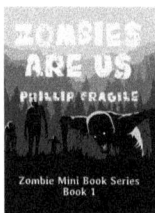

Zombies Are Us
2021 ISBN: 978-1-77354-338-3

Available at PageMaster Publishing
pagemasterpublishing.ca/by/phillip-fragile/

Phillip Fragile

How to
Get Out
of a
Mental
Hospital

HOW TO GET OUT OF A MENTAL HOSPITAL
Copyright © Phillip Fragile, 2022

Published by Phillip Fragile, Edmonton, Canada

ISBN:
Paperback   978-1-77354-412-0
Ebook   978-1-77354-413-7

Publication assistance by

PAGEMASTER
PUBLISHING
PageMaster.ca

CONTENTS

one

Calm Down

Control your actions and be polite.

If you offend people, is your treatment going to be bearable? This is something that I had to figure out. It is as if no one is there to help you. I just was so offended by people and they knew that. If I had been calm and polite, it would have shaved a lifetime off of my stay. No one told me and I didn't get it.

It is easy to be kind to a kind person. It is easy to treat someone well if they are nice. Be a kind person. If you are viewed as a problem, you are never getting out. And stick with it. In time, their view of you will change.

Sometimes you need to change. Are you argumentative? Are you throwing up red flags? Do you talk about vulgar things? Do you use swear words in every conversation? A calm and polite person does none of this. It doesn't even matter what your illness is, if you keep yourself in check. Do not be intimidating. They should never have to wonder if you are going to lash out. This doesn't sound fair, but in a mental hospital, they will treat you restrictively based on how you make them feel, not necessarily on your actions.

Have a good reputation. Stay calm in the face of adversity. Be calm and be fine with whatever you are facing. If they tell you that no one can visit you, you have to be fine. If they tell you that you can't smoke, you have to be fine. If they told you that they are letting you go, then change their statement, you have to be fine. You will handle it. You are fine. Otherwise you could fade eternity in a box. Some people don't get out. Be ice under fire.

Another part of watching what you say, is not putting out red flags. A, "red flag," is the term someone uses for behaviors that are a warning to staff that you may be a problem. If you put up a red flag, they will write it in your chart and they will talk about it. This is risky behavior. Talking about risky behavior is not being calm, however, thinking about risky behavior tends to come out. You will be found out. This applies to all people you talk to. If you have something hidden in your mind, it tends to come out under pressure.

It is a red flag to talk about running away. It is a red flag to talk about crime or violence. Leave your past in your past. Don't talk about risky behavior. You cannot talk about caring about or anything sexual about someone who works there.

You will see a lot of people who send out warning signs or red flags. Even if they don't seem to get in trouble. Even if you have no one to talk to. There are times in life when you feel you need the right person to talk to. Well, you have this book. If you follow me, better is on it's way. I got out of impossible. You can too.

This is pretty much the most important thing - staying calm no matter what. I had tried listening to their way. Do this and this, and you'll be free. But I found that if I listened, freedom was no where in sight. It was like I was going in circles. And I found that it is not a good idea to rely on them. No one told me what to think. You would think that in a mental hospital, that they would tell you how to think. You have to represent you. No one is going to save you. You have to master yourself. And well, I'm here for you.

You could have done or been through something scary. But if you get the reputation of being calm and gentle, this is a reputation that you are a, "safe person."

When I first could barely grasp that I was out of control, I put myself through a life change. Even though I had disturbing voices and nightmares, I was in control. It took two years of me really searching, for me to rebuild myself. But the whole time, I was calm.

I began by being too submissive. I let other patients verbally abuse me. I didn't stand up for myself. I wasn't even assertive. I was very pushy before. I would let anybody who opposed me know, that I wouldn't put up with disrespect. I would fight anyone. I had to turn all that back.

I have found that being nice is stronger. I can be a little mean once in a while, but I am nice to everyone. I don't care what they've done. They could have been the worst. Don't trust everyone, but forgive everyone. Holding a grudge is only hard on you. And you don't want to be snapping. You don't want to have built up rage. Forgive. And I know they do messed up things to people in mental hospitals. Some people shouldn't be around vulnerable people.

Now that you are peaceful calm and polite, they can move you forward. Don't get worked up, don't get excited. I have found it best to actually be in the moment. Don't waste your thoughts. What is your purpose? What gives meaning? Be a light! There are people there that will never have more. Be kind to them. Lift their spirits. Do that with staff too. Carry peace. You can do that by not looking for approval. Don't try to be cool. Just know you are. Don't try to convince anyone anything. Be the truth. Be the way. Calmness is a well trained pupil. A very physically able person can show fierce control of their peace. If people say things to you to bring you down, don't become down. If someone called you a clown, would you believe them? Are you a clown? So let them see that they didn't insult you by the way you look. If it bothers you, they will do it again. If they don't take your peace, all they have are their words ringing in their ears that were uncalled for. Leave them to reflect on themselves because their insult didn't work. Just carry on being you. And you believe in you. I believe in you. You are doing your best.

If they come at you with a bunch of tasks that you can't handle, it's ok to say that you can't. Whatever is placed in front of you, be fine with, but if you can't, you can't.

When I got to hospital, they wouldn't let us sleep in or stay in our rooms. If we stepped in our rooms, they would lock us in. They would be physical if they found someone sleeping on the floor. But, if you can stay in your room, you avoid a lot of drama. Removing yourself from situations relieves options for failure. People are saying things that potentially cause trouble? Room. People don't appreciate you? Room.

I will try to mention what someone acts like who doesn't have peace. Someone who doesn't have control. This person is constantly stating what the problems are. This person is not fine with it. You never know what this person will do or say. They often do or say things that have shock value. This person talks about voices. This person says how special they are. This person talks about the true significance of their hallucinations. This person will be violent if someone insults them. This person will be violent because of a voice or a hallucination. This person talks to themselves. This person laughs audibly when no one is around. This person doesn't think much of the here and now. This person thinks that they are master of some universe. This person is not calm.

You will do great. Believe that. Don't get carried away and act normal. Just think of a normal polite person from the outside world who doesn't have mental illness and you'll be fine. Not someone who gets away with stuff, not an antisocial person (criminal, drug user etc.) with this writing you have everything you need. Be patient. A couple months or years could be a lot worse. This, in my writing, is the most simple way. If someone would have taught me this information, I wouldn't have been such a wreck. I was vulnerable and needed a way. They say it's up to you to get out. It's like there was no way out.. Everything led me in circles and lies. They do things to see how you react. It may look bad, but be a straight arrow. Fly in one direction towards the bulls eye. Be unshakeable. Meds can feel very bad. Accept what you need to accept.

Mental illness just means we think differently. We are a people. We can do this together. We are beautiful.

Two

Dealing with Staff and Doctors

Being in a caring environment seems important.

You are deemed as a threat to yourself or others. That's why you are here. If you are not in a caring environment, be a caring environment. Sometimes people will be nice to you and make you feel safe when you are not safe. Some people propose good things to get something. Don't be one of these people.

Nurses, doctors and staff are not your friends. They can act friendly and they will often listen and write down their perceptions afterwards. I have had many things written down about me and not necessarily true things either. Be the same person in front of everyone.

I have found that being nice to a mean person is one of the most rewarding things. A mean person may show their meanness right away. A nice person may show that they are kind of nice right away, only to get nicer as time goes on. But being kind to a mean person as time goes on, they may become kind of nice, like the nice person was right away! When someone is toxic, I stay away from them and don't trust them. But I am still nice to them when I see them.

When talking to staff, don't try and get them to believe something. State things like facts when people ask if it's appropriate. If you try and make a doctor believe something, I have found, that he gives you medication. If you don't know how to think, I have found, he or she writes a prescription. I have not heard a doctor say, "Everyone has messed up thoughts sometimes. The brain doesn't listen to instruction. If you tell yourself not to think of a pink elephant, you will. Trying to forget, you won't. Don't be shocked by your own mind. Just move along." That would have helped me a lot to know. But if you are mentally ill, people seem to skip the simple instruction, even if that is all that's needed.

Sometimes, when I was placed on a new medication, I would have so much trouble dealing with it that I would appear strange. Then I would get more and appear worse. This was a harmful cycle for me.

They aren't allowed to be your friend. This is what is considered by them to be unprofessional. They could lose what job security they have. You would probably speak differently to your friends, am I right? Would you completely trust someone who doesn't benefit from talking to you other than money? If you are not doing well or guarding secrets with them, it goes into their reports. Be normal. These are professional relationships. These people are doing their job. Their relationships that really know them are their family and friends.

I am not hallucinating or hearing voices anymore on my medication. It took years on the same drug for this to happen. But while I was, I did not listen to voices or hallucinations while I was doing ok. The doctor often wants to get rid of the voice. It is just a part of your brain.

I have found it best not to get my hopes up. I have found it best to not rely on what I'm getting told. I have found that people lie.

I have found that people play mind games. I do not call them out on it. I don't talk about it. I just observe. If I am told that I am getting privileges, or that I am being released, I don't really believe it until I see it. If I don't get worked up, then I don't get let down if it was false. I have found that I was let down so many times that I became numb. I had the 100 yard stare. Like I only saw what was in front of me.

Mental hospitals can be a place of nightmares. You need to stay calm. If you are poked, keep your peace. If you are manipulated, don't loose your composure. If you are lied to or about, breathe. They wrote some pretty horrific things about me that weren't true. I felt publicly humiliated. Still I rise. Still I got out. I maintained me. I mastered myself. Now I have such peace.

When I see the doctor, I know that he is looking for information. I know that what he says about me and how he treats me is important. I don't try and get him to believe something. I do my best to be calm. I am not raising alarms. In regular life I try to be symptom mild. My medication works. I think all mentally ill have strange thinking. I don't get wound up in strange thinking. I can let go of what I see and hear because I know I'm mentally ill. Everybody has some messed up thoughts sometimes. I don't try to forget. I am ok with myself.

My doctor said at 2 of my review board hearings (they gather with me about once a year to see how I'm doing, grant or take away freedoms) that I didn't believe that I was mentally ill, when that wasn't true. What he had said to me to base this off of was in the form of a question. Did I believe that my mental illness was a problem. I had said no, because I could manage. He said that if my mental illness wasn't a problem, then it was unexplained phenomena. Don't base your case on this, but some talks seem so tricky.

The more you talk about your delusions, the more confused you are. And if you believe them, it's not like you are going to forget them. The things that come out of your mouth often are what you focus on, but you tend to focus on them more if you talk about them. I have found it mostly best to defuse my delusions myself over time. Something I've always done is keep a journal. I have notes from when I was nothing but a red flag. But it doesn't matter how many red flags are in your head. It matters what you do and say. A mentally ill person that talks and acts like a normal person is doing well, I would say. I would have a regular well day, but in my head I would be going through so many different feelings. Take my anxiety medications, come for my injection and know that it helps me and life is good. I don't even think about those things much as I present as calm, collected and cool. The things that give me purpose is being positive, talking about my faith, praying for people and talking about mental illness. The more I can encourage people and lift their spirits, the less weight there is in the room. If I can bring joy into someone's day, people are going to see better. I don't preach to people. I don't try and make them believe. I don't point out their errors. But if they look to me, I am alright. I carry peace. I do my best to be a good influence. I tell people what I have if they ask. I say we are mentally ill. I do not say you are mentally ill. I say when we are delusional, not you. I feel that I can really speak up about mental illness because I am mentally ill.

Being in control is the most important. Staying away from people as they get into trouble is important. Speaking about positive things or just being positive is like a life line for some people. Telling nurses and doctors the importance of my mental health, that I need to be prosocial, in control and sharing with staff is what I need to do. Remember to say sorry and thank you often to everybody like you mean it. Present yourself as you are safe. Be safe. They are looking to see if you are a danger to yourself or others. Be safe even if no one sees it. Don't build up beliefs in your head. Be calm inside too.

Three

Mental Illness? What You Don't Get

Your average Joe doesn't believe everything that passes through his mind.

Be average Joe. There are people all over that believe that they are the One on some cosmic plan. After I was in a hospital for a very long time, I saw this. I thought that I was the great important, only way the universe was going to be ok. If I had seen that this was common, if I understood it, I could have sized down my beliefs. And it does provide a surge inside with such beliefs. It makes you colossal inside. It feels fun. With such purpose, I felt like I could do anything. Mentally ill people do scary things believing like this. Remember that you need to master yourself. You need to know what is really happening. The more you see things as they are, the wiser you are.

Mental illness is our brand. It does not feel good to be labeled. Especially with hatred. If people hate us, it's because they don't know us. I do my best to show how much we can shine. I will say I'm mentally ill just to stand up for us. I am nice to all of our kin and I don't care what they did. I don't say, "At least I'm not that guy." I will be nice to that guy. I am strong. And my strength is shown with great control. Anything could be going through my head, yet I am the same.

Being mentally ill is something I had and have to tell myself. Being delusional means believing something not normal. I can get caught up in a string of thoughts and not get too lost. If I get a little confused, I don't judge myself. Being a little confused and very confused is night and day. Being a little confused is ok. I am ok with being a little different. I stay away from very. If you are very confused you can hit the bottom. Some people don't come back. They go and get lost in another world, and that is how they demise.

Be careful that you are not deceived. To not know what is real, is like not being. If you barely wonder if you are mentally ill, grab that thought. Make it real. This is what you need to survive. Concentrate hard for weeks until it stays. To forever be in loops is not good. Be constant.

People all around the hospital believe it's not them deep down. They end up losing what freedom they have because their illness brings them back. It's like they are happy believing they have no issue and then end up in a snare. They get confused just enough that they do the wrong thing, then believe that it won't happen again. This time. They will get out for good this time. I was wrong over and over, in the same loop, and I didn't change. "If only they would see," I thought. What I really needed was a life change. I needed to know I am mentally ill. I could have let go of things. I could have been more aware of my condition. How we are. Staying well.

Staying well doesn't feel that good at first. You have to go through knots of thoughts and keep untangling them with your new tool. I am mentally ill. That knowledge is my tool. A lot of those knots gave me purpose. A lot of those knots were entertaining. I remember thinking life was better when I was delusional.

So many people, in mental hospitals, that did or are doing something strange, believe that they are not mentally ill. The, "No way, God is real." Or, "I really am this special." No one should be there to tell you that you aren't special, or that God isn't real. God cares about you so much and you are so special. God is with people. God puts callings on people's lives. I do my best. But the way that I think is different. I have to let go of a lot. My weird or strange thinking can get the best of me if I don't use my tool. I am mentally ill. I will do great things for God. But they won't be violent. They won't be vengeance. They won't be weird. I am going to be a good influence. We are supposed to share the gospel. The Bible says that those who believe will have signs accompanying them. That they will cast out demons, cleanse the lepers, raise the dead and lay hands on the sick and they shall recover. Now if you are praying for people to be healed, that's what they do at church. Not all churches though. My weird thinking was believing things that weren't in the Bible. Or believing that I was special in a different way. I let go of a lot of things. If people in church feel something, they will check by one or two different people in the church community that also feel the same thing. I see people in church who feel that they have something from God, but they also know that they could have gotten it wrong. They don't want to be false. They check with other people who also have a relationship with Jesus. For me, my relationship with Jesus is that I feel loved, I feel that God is proud of me and I feel that I am doing my best. But you will see me praying for someone sometimes. This is just my experience. This is what it means to me to be a believer.

Some people's delusions are different. Mine were about the Bible or aliens. I am correct-able. A lot of people believe someone can read their mind and things like telepathy. Or that someone alive or dead is talking to them. Maybe a celebrity. I have thought that a celebrity was communicating with me before. This is all strange and people who are mentally ill don't see it. They believe everything that comes to their heads. They don't believe that they could ever be wrong. A person who believes that they have a relationship with Jesus, knows that he/ she could be wrong about what they feel in a particular instance. It is very important that we are not deceived.

When you have view points that are normal in the community and you are not obsessed with being 100% right, these things can still be considered strange. Everything I've written here can be considered strange. But I am trying to express mental illness and what some people think is normal. If I get a little confused it's ok. To be very confused and acting on it is not ok.

Hospital Drawings

Expression is art. Art is expression. In these days and times, you must not be a concern. Be polite. Be gentle. The rest is up to them.

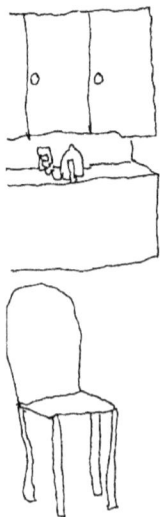

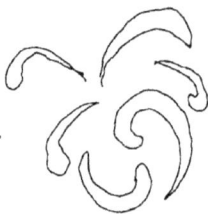

Phillip Fragile

You can not rely on what you hear and see and feel. Knowing you are mentally ill means you don't over focus.

Phillip
Fragile

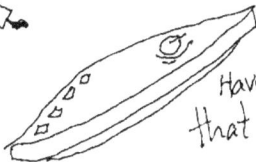

Have you heard
that the space
in your mind is
☆ Limitless? ☆

Them needles'll get you every time! And those NINJAS! They would out number 8 foot tall muscle bound Sasquatches!

Phillip Fragile

In the days of the Black Mask
there were many people
just surviving. But the
Black Mask was comfort.
Almost like a comfort
blanket. The People
needed peace
within themselves.
Medication and
learning seemed
to be the way.
How do I act?
What do I say?
We must be in
control...

Phillip
Fragile 2006

Phillip
Fragile

Hesitation in the mind is for thought
before speach. Have a set of
rules you use to conduct
yourself. AKA Always be polite.
Never act or speak in
agression. If you can control
your actions peacefully...

Instead of being nice all the time and hiding your anger until you snap, be a little bit mean sometimes...

Phillip Fragile

Four
Exercise and Medication

I am on the right medication.

I suffered a lot with it.

I have felt the worst. I have felt the lowest low. I have told a doctor I was scared because my vision was askew on the new med. So he decided to increase my dose. I have been afraid. I have had my eyes roll back in my skull. (That is called oculogyric crisis. One of the symptoms is terror.) I have begged. I have cried. But if I don't take my meds, I am not in control. I can get lost on one concern. Then there are voices and hallucinations that magically seem like truth. When it is very important that we are not deceived. You don't want to be a lost person. You don't want to perish.

I experienced so much terror that I used to wish that I just felt bad like the others. Because bad can slowly return to normal. I felt really bad on the right medication. The one where I could be careful and take my actions seriously. With the right steps, I now feel normal. My food tastes good and I can even go for a run and have energy through the day. People can't tell that I am mentally ill.

They have injections that go in the butt or arm that lasts weeks or a month. I am happy that I am on the right drug and it's great that it goes in my arm. People often go through a struggle after a needle. I don't. I do some cardio after my needle. If you take antipsychotics (that's what the meds are called) and you don't move much, meds can make you feel pretty bad.

When I take any antipsychotic medication my brain goes into duress. I get episodes of anxiety so bad that when I go there, I forget how terrible it can be. This only would happen if I didn't take a small dose eight hours apart morning and evening of an antianxiety medication. I had suffered for years and suddenly I came up with this and it worked, it wasn't the doctor's idea, but he went along with it. When it worked, I couldn't stop laughing. I had been suffering for hours every second day.

They also have oral medication. This would have the same feeling on a regular basis, but they would often prefer to give us needles so that they can be sure we are not hiding our meds and spitting them out. Injection or oral, whatever works for you, find the right med. This can be a struggle.

Now. You may have tried medication. You may hate medication. You may have experienced some bad side effects. But... if you get carried away and into a reality that you act on, medication is the only way. Sometimes the hard way is the right way.

Even if you don't exercise, do a little after your shot. If you wait until it hits you, it is very difficult to exercise when you feel bad. Get the blood circulating.

I have found that after a long time on meds, that when I worked out, I would feel worse for a day. I did a hard exercise and it was as if I had to detox. If I am not mistaken, meds can build up in your fat cells. After a good 3 or 4 times, I felt good. I kept my mood to myself.

Now, when I do my exercise, a rapid walk for 30 minutes and 10 minutes at the punching bag keeps me from feeling trapped in a bad feeling. And sometimes a bunch of jumping jacks will get my blood flowing enough to feel better if I feel muddled up. Now you may not have a punching bag where you are, but you can do some sort of exercise that gets your heart beating.

At first, when I was having trouble coping, I would take a PRN (Pro Re Nata?) This is Latin I think for as needed. If they don't call it that, it's just a drug you can ask for and is not your regular medication. It is not scheduled as a med that you need to take on a regular basis. Some pills you may take may make you feel alright to relax. And well, I used these more, until I discovered exercise. The first time I was going to take my as needed medication, but I thought I would see what a run did first.

At first I really pushed my cardio exercise. Cardio just means exercise that makes you breathe harder for more than 20 minutes. I ran really hard for an hour to keep me from becoming too dismal. Then I found out that I didn't need that much. I feel about the same all the time now. I feel good.

The other thing that I need is anxiety medication. I have found that myself and others can get symptoms even and episodes that seem terrible. It is amazing that I found I can take a medication that is not an antipsychotic, that is considered addictive twice a day and I don't get episodes. I suffered for a long time in a terrible way before I discovered this. Now, if I forget to take my pills, it is like I feel one of these episodes closer. I don't notice anything now, but when I first took them I felt a little tired immediately after. This went away, but if I forget to take them, I will have trouble sleeping. This is just what I do and by no means is this expert or clinical advice. This is from my experiences as a patient, not as a nurse or doctor.

Five

Being Deemed as Inappropriate. You Have Feelings for Someone? The Truth Will Come Out

You may think it's harmless to have a crush on someone.

But staff members, nurses and doctors are a no go. They will call you inappropriate. So you keep your feelings inside? They will write whatever they want about you. They could make you look very strange. Do not care about them. You may be lonely. You may feel like you have no one in the world. They may appear friendly. They may help you. But don't count on them.

The doctor may tell you not to talk to a person that is friendly to you. Don't talk to them. Avoid them. Stay on the straight and narrow. They could perceive something innocent as a problem. You don't want them to label you. You don't want them against you. Just be nice to everyone and don't have desire for them. Don't keep it inside. Feelings come out. If they change your treatment, you don't want it to be rationalized by something that has nothing to do with mental illness. Staying calm is easier if you don't have a flow of emotions. A lot of what they do can seem unfair.

You can also be deemed as inappropriate just by saying or doing things that are more normal outside of the hospital. Don't talk about sexual things or say vulgar things. A person who is out of control is non-stop in this department. A little joke not at the expense of others once in a while is more acceptable than pointing towards someone. You want them to say positive things about you. You want to be simple. To get everyone more or less on your side, stay away from saying or doing things that could make people insecure. If you say something sexual about one of them, you may be moved to another area or one of the staff members may be removed. Any relationship talk may also do the same thing.

If or when you lose control and they place you in a room you could end up in distress and say you love someone. They may keep you in that room. When I was placed in a room, I didn't know how to get out. I didn't stay calm. My beard and nails grew. They would force extra one time drugs on me that I was terrified of. Being alone and terrified, I said and did things that were humiliating. They have their charts and were taking copious notes.

I had suicidal thoughts in abundance while in hospital. I hit rock bottom. I could have hardly imagined that someone could live in those conditions. Some patients don't make it out alive. Going for a walk on hospital property seeing something like a rope hanging from a tree in the bush wasn't an abnormal thing to see there. You may want to be out of there so badly. You will make it. Some people never figure it out. Life can be so serious. I survived through the worst. No one told me I needed to stay at peace. When your world comes crashing down it is honorable to keep your cool.

Make it through mental illness. Be the person who cares even if no one else does. Be appropriate, be constant and when you fall, get back up again.

Six

Do You Know What They Mean by Delusional?

Being different is ok.

Being different is cool. I believe we are our own people. We are in the class of mentally ill. We have our own culture. Mentally ill people can be the worst. But we can also be the best. There is nothing wrong with being mentally ill. We are different. Different is good. If you tell people from the outside world about your illness, they tend to run. Let them.

People that never get out of hospital, or keep returning to hospital, don't really believe that they are mentally ill, they believe that other people are, but not them. This means that they can't say to themselves, "I should probably let that go. It seems real, but I am mentally ill."

And since they don't really believe that they are mentally ill, they believe everything that goes through their heads. So they go to hospital when their illness decides, as it were.

I believed that I was the only one. My delusions made me the biggest person in the world. A delusion is believing that which others don't, for the most part. Like for example, that you are the reincarnated Bruce Lee. Like believing you can create things by making them appear. I have met many people who believed that they were Jesus or God. Believing in, "only you," is going to lose you. You could get lost in schizophrenia. You could just go on a trip and never realize reality. Knowing what is going on is mastering yourself. The more accurately you perceive yourself and where you are, the more wisdom you have and if you can see in the most simple way, this is the most accurate. Remember. We are mentally ill. Others use that word as an insult. Let's take what they called us and make it beautiful. We experience more than they do.

Even though I went through the seemingly impossible process of finding the right medication, I still tell myself that I am mentally ill. Even though my symptoms are better, I still have strange thinking. I still let things go.

They have your room to lock you in or another. When you are out of control, or they think you are. I have found myself locked in these rooms unto a state of oblivion. I was on another planet as they forgot about me in the real world. I think when we can be by ourselves for too long we can deteriorate a lot more. One of these times as I remember, was because I had said the wrong thing. A lot is expected out of us. We are responsible for taming our illness. A lot can go on in our heads, but it's about what we let out in our decisions.

It's like we are cast into a storm and we need to find our way back. Picking up the pieces and choosing the right examples is important. So let's look at the person you want to be:

This person is cool in the fire. This person doesn't cause any alarm. This person doesn't shock anyone. This person is predictable. If there is suspected drug use, it isn't this person. This person is polite. He or she is easy to talk to. This person doesn't try to talk to someone who doesn't want to talk. This person found the right medication. When this person talks to doctors, nurses or staff, he or she isn't trying to convince them that they are ok. This person is ok. They don't try and make others believe. This person has their beliefs and answers questions if asked. Someone can see this person is doing well because of the peace that they have.

Being delusional or mentally ill and being aware of yourself or having insight starts with how you view yourself, think and talk about yourself. Saying something that you kind of realize you shouldn't believe and adding, "I know this is a delusion," is a starting place. Sometimes just recognizing the way you think, or knowing what is strange, is a start. By saying, "But this might be a delusion," opens your mind more. Reality or the perception of such, is negotiable in your mind. If something is true, having thoughts that question it, will prove it even more. If it is true. Being mentally ill or delusional and knowing it took work. I would have the thought that, "What if I'm delusional/mentally ill," once in a while, but I never pursued it. I didn't have a look at everything that I could perceive. But when I finally got it, I had to reinforce it by telling myself over and over. It was critical. I had to concentrate.

Seven

The Best Peace I Have Ever Heard of

Got a Bible? This chapter may not be for everyone.

I mention the "J" word.

Happiness isn't extreme pleasure. If you go way up, you go way down. Having peace, being content and satisfaction is happiness. Feeling good on a regular basis is happiness. Letting go of wants for things you don't have right now brings a small satisfaction. Small satisfactions build into soothing relief. Knowing that there is a great plan for you and that you are truly loved is where it's at. I have found these things with Jesus.

To steadily be on your course and knowing that no weapon formed against you will prosper comes with Jesus. I carry a peace with me wherever I go because I am blessed. Jesus lives in me and if you invite him in and give your life to him, that's it! You are his life. He will help you. Just do your best to follow him, keep setting your mind to do right by him (repenting) and believe that he was crucified and rose from the grave and ascended into heaven and you've got him! He came from God and is God and the way. I see it is like this:

Father God made his family (angels.) Some of them didn't appreciate living in the radiance of love with their perfect immortal bodies. They turned against the One who made them led by Lucifer. So, in God's universe, everything had been given to them. So God made Earth with a trial period for us to see if we would choose our family and love. Jesus came from this other place to break us away from death and show us the way. God came to us in the form of a Man. If we choose our family with our Heavenly Father through this life, then we get our perfect, invincible, immortal bodies and paradise. Because some souls are twisted. Some only destroy everything eventually. Lest you be deceived, for there is Hell.

Jesus is here to be our companion. To be friends with us. Holy spirit is there to teach us.

Father God is here to be our heart. We lack something if we don't complete what we were made for. That bond with God. He gave us desire to fulfill that desire.

Now. You may have skipped this chapter, but these are the keys. With Jesus looking out for us, we can do the right thing!

Eight
Street Drugs, Alcohol and Running Away

Do you need a break from suffering?

There are things in life that you should be afraid of. There are situations that you don't want to be in. And there are things that are "bad" too. Being bad is different than being terrible. There are people that do things that are forgivable, even if they are not so hot. Then there is destruction. Loss of life. You don't want to be this person.

The staff, doctors and a large part of society could turn away from you. They could view you as someone to be avoided. Someone they are scared to let their family see. Someone headed for destruction. Someone that may destroy others. And if you have already become a drug addict, don't give up! For this is a fight for your life! If you have fear of being a drug addict, this is good. If you fear what happens to the severe alcoholics this is good. Someone like a judge is going to view someone who drinks a few beers and smokes some pot a lot different than someone who does meth or cocaine, heroine or someone who lives off of hard alcohol.

The hospital that sees you mess up and smoke a joint is going to punish you but still have hope for you. But if the hospital sees that you are doing meth, you are that red flag. I have seen people who use meth. I have hung out with them. They were all over the place. Then I go to try and see how they are doing and find out they are dead. Cocaine too. If you can survive this. If you can realize that cravings eventually go away. If you have survived mental illness or drugs, you have found the grace of God. Wow. Good on you for making it out.

If you run away from hospital, there is a very long record on your hands. If you take off and get away there is almost no chance of you making it more than a week. There have been people who do longer than that, but they are living dangerously. All these people end up trapped inside the hospital for a very long time. Years pass. If someone runs away and does hard drugs or gets really drunk and they find them, they are facing hardship. But if someone runs away and has a couple beers and turns themselves in, they are facing less punishment. There is a lot less hardship for that person who realizes they messed up and comes back.

But doing any drugs or drinking, or even talking about it is a red flag. This is not the way to mental wellness and getting out of hospital. If you plan to do it when you are free, it will probably come out of you, in actions or words before you are free. Exit the damaging cycle. Live a life free from something others are trapped in. To set a plan into action and make life changes to freedom and wholeness is living drug and alcohol free. Free. That is a good word.

Nine

People Who Encourage You. Your People

When I got to hospital, I had no friends. This really took a toll on me. When I was facing hardship, I had no one in my corner. I had no one to tell me to relax and that I was going to be ok. I didn't know how to think or act. The doctor said to trust him. This was the way out he said. I was vulnerable. He said, do I have voices. I told him the first thing that came to mind when he asked me if I heard anything bad. I had stated the things that I thought were the worst. He wrote them down and they are still mentioned in my chart. I had tried to be honest. But I had misunderstood. When I was asked if I was a danger to myself or others I had said I could think of the worst dangers right now. What he had wanted to know was if I had regularity dwelt on had things. Not if I could think of them when prompted. I didn't have advice for common sense.

Other people that I talked to were patients that were considered a risk. One patient told me that the way out of the hospital was to refuse my medication. I did. Then the hospital took away my rights. They would use police, security guards or others to physically force injections on me. I was terrified and I had no one to talk to. I would have gone right through my hospital stay if I had just known that all I had to do was stay peaceful, polite and calm. No one told me. I could find no one I could trust. I was out of control and my mouth was running. I was in an emergency situation with no one at my side. The words of this book are at your side. Say and do normal. Don't look at celebrities and rowdy behavior as the way to be. Think of a normal quiet person. I couldn't find an appropriate role model or peer.

There are people you can trust. But you are going to scare them away if you don't talk to them right. People allow you in their lives. You are paying rent with them by treating them well. If you are not giving people their space, they can abandon you because the people who allow you in their life need to be comfortable in your relationship with them. When someone says back off, back off. If someone doesn't want to talk to you, give them all the space and time they need. If you have a friend who is comfortable with you, and you can trust them, you have what you need. You can stay relatively normal if you can have regular healthy relationships. Or you can practice at least. When you call people you won't be the person that they don't know how to handle.

Having positive people in your life is awesome. Someone who tells you that you can do it and that they believe in you. Even if you only talk to them once in a while. These are support people. These are people that don't gossip about you. These are people you can trust with your well being. But how are you going to have or keep these people if you repeatedly call them and they don't feel comfortable answering? Calm down, you are fine. There is true value in talking to someone once in a while.

There are different types of people. There are those who truly have your best interests at heart, and those who do not. Let's first talk about those who do not.

They are there to talk to. They may not make you feel the best about yourself, but they talk to you for them. They talk about you to other people. You make them look good. They may feel good for you to hang around with. They make you think that they are cool. But they will constantly do things that end up deteriorating your life. You trust them because you can't seem to notice that they destroy. They put you down so that you look up to them. There are people who are just toxic. They look and act cool. But that is all they have. They make a joke or make fun of a helpless person. They lead you to bad choices. They are there to set you up and to trick you.

A good person is different and a good person may still look and act cool. The pure of heart. Someone who picks you up when you are down. Someone who tells you that you are great, just keep putting one foot in front of the other. You can trust this person and they keep your secrets. You've just got to treat them right. You can make mistakes and they put up with you when you are a little off. You build this relationship with consistency over time.

You will find your team, your tribe. Some people may have been removed from your life. You may wish to talk to them again. But some things happen for a reason. You will find your people. And if you are missing someone in your life, be that person to others. Be there for people, encourage those that don't have anyone. You can relate to a lot of emotions that you've been through. Loss, loneliness, devastation and maybe even heartache.

I had a group of friends that I would stay away from now. Some people aren't good for your lives. Some people stick together to cause trouble. Maybe have friends that may have been through some things but still have hope. Like I said, some people seem to only be there to destroy.

Be nice to people. Brighten things up in a dark place. Carry peace. Some people may reject you if you are looking for their approval. Sometimes it is better to say less. Just be who you are. I put up with a lot if I find someone is annoying. I don't complain about people. Some people regularly talk down of others or their illness. Some people get their entertainment value from hating or making fun of someone. Don't be this person. Say hi to everyone. Ask them how they are. Don't lend out the things you need and lend like you are giving and don't expect back. Some people need a mom or a dad. You can teach others how to act by being a good example.

To have someone you can trust to talk to is golden. Someone who is consistently in your life as a blessing is amazing. I have found that before I found my people that someone would show up like a light. They seemed to understand me and see the real me. These people were gems in my life. They weren't the same people, they weren't consistent people. But they were stepping stones in my life to remember when I had no one. When I was alone feeling destroyed. Sometimes there is no help and life just drags on. It can feel like that locked in a room in a hospital. Use my words. If you want something someone has, try doing things their way.

Ten

Leaving Hospital. Going Out Into the Crowds

It may be a simple transition. It may be the time that makes things right. Finally. For me when I was getting out of hospital, I was ready. I didn't get too excited. I didn't have trouble sleeping with anticipation. I didn't even feel that sure that I was actually leaving the hospital. I just believe things as I see them. So many times I've had my hopes crushed. So then I wouldn't get my hopes up about anything. If you go way up, you go way down. So I try to keep things even.

Some people can't handle getting out of the hospital. There are feelings that can come. You may feel very alone. Everything may feel lifeless. You may find yourself overwhelmed by large groups of people. Some people stop taking their medication and end up back in hospital. Some people turn to street drugs and end up back in hospital or jail. Try to do things evenly. Don't go too up or too down. Take your meds. Shower. Do chores. Talk to your psychiatrist.

For a long time I knew that I was better. I remembered who I used to be as a kid, when I was easily understood, I had a good reputation and I said and did the things I meant to. I became this person again. I honestly express myself. It is easier to see who I am because I honestly express myself. I think we all have a memory of ourselves when we were truly ourselves. Not an isolated incident. When life was bright for a season. I was this person, then in my teenage years I had a lot of drive to be someone and I lost my simple self. When I became mentally ill, I became someone else. When I was sick I wasn't me. I wasn't me for a long time. When I did a life change and was calm and polite, I began to recognize myself again. When people could notice my emotions more easily. Peaceful emotions. Peaceful attitude.

Getting out into the community is better. It feels more human not being locked up. But I also had peace in the hospital when I was well for the end of my stay.

But getting out of the hospital takes work. Life changes and having insight to your illness is real. If you have read this book, you have the way. Put your head through all this and if people don't seem to notice you've changed, keep it up. It may be fun to be out of control, but to get out and leave hospital, you need to put yourself in gear. And stay in gear. Do this for the amount of time it takes. I had a bad reputation. I had to show the new me until everybody that mattered got it. The process seemed slow. Even if no one believes in you, you believe in you. Go through the process to leave hospital. Don't just think suddenly you are better now and expect everyone to hop to it. It is a lifestyle. Be the real you again. Stay in that mindset.

Phillip Fragile at PageMaster Publishing
https://pagemasterpublishing.ca/by/phillip-fragile/

To order more copies of this book, find books by
other Canadian authors, or make inquiries about
publishing your own book, contact PageMaster at:

PageMaster Publication Services Inc.
11340-120 Street, Edmonton, AB T5G 0W5
books@pagemaster.ca
780-425-9303

catalogue and e-commerce store
PageMasterPublishing.ca/Shop

www.ingramcontent.com/pod-product-compliance
Lightning Source LLC
Chambersburg PA
CBHW071932020426
42331CB00010B/2837